Bible Exploration for High School
A Two-Year Course

Student Workbook
Year 1

Ron Cohen

Brilliant Jewel Press

Bible Exploration for High School
Student Workbook—Year 1

Copyright © 2015 Brilliant Jewel Press
All rights reserved.

Scripture quotations are taken from the New American Standard Bible®,
Copyright © 1960, 1962, 1963, 1968, 1971, 1972, 1973, 1975, 1977, 1995 by The Lockman Foundation. Used by permission. (www.Lockman.org).

Scripture quotations marked (NLT) are taken from the *Holy Bible*, New Living Translation, copyright © 1996, 2004, 2007 by Tyndale House Foundation. Used by permission of Tyndale House Publishers, Inc., Carol Stream, Illinois 60188. All rights reserved.

Scripture quotations marked (KJV) are from the King James Version.

Reproduction or translation of any part of this work beyond that permitted by Section 107 and 108 of the 1976 United States Copyright Act without the written permission of the copyright owner is unlawful. Requests for permission or other information must be secured from the publisher.

Brilliant Jewel Press
30141 Antelope Road #D-601
Menifee CA 92584
www.brilliantjewelpress.com

www.explorethebiblebook.com

(Student workbooks with coil bindings, which open flat, can be ordered from either web site.)

Printed in the United States of America.

ISBN: 978-0-69238-483-1   Paperback
       978-1-63315-889-4   CD

Table of Contents

Semester 1 Kick Off...1
    Unit 1: Beginnings 3
    Unit 2: Israel in Egypt 5
    Unit 3: Matthew 7
    Unit 4: Israel at Sinai 10
    Unit 5: Sentenced to the Desert 12
    Unit 6: Mark 14
    Unit 7: Preparation for Conquest 17
    Unit 8: Inheritance Realized 20
    Unit 9: Luke 22
Semester 1 Exam 25
Semester 2 Kick Off 29
    Unit 10: When the Judges Governed 31
    Unit 11: Job 33
    Unit 12: John 36
    Unit 13: Samuel and Saul 39
    Unit 14: David 41
    Unit 15: Acts 45
    Unit 16: Solomon 48
    Unit 17: Proverbs 51
    Unit 18: Romans 54
Semester 2 Exam..58

Semester 1
Activities

1. **Calendar:** Create a monthly calendar depicting scenes of creation. For the scenes, collect or take photos, or make drawings.

2. **Review:** Watch the classic movie <u>The Ten Commandments</u> (1956), by Cecil B. DeMille. Write a review of the movie; include writing, acting, direction, cinematography, etc. How closely were the Scriptures followed, and were there major departures? Do you give the movie a "thumbs up" or a "thumbs down"?

3. **Maps:** Draw one or more maps depicting the course the Hebrews followed to conquer Canaan. Include the major battles and how the land was distributed afterward.

4. **Interview:** Interview some senior citizens who have been believers for many years. What have they witnessed? What is their advice to younger believers? Be prayerful and sensitive about your questions and be respectful of their answers.

5. **Report:** Prepare a written report discussing the major issues of creationism vs. evolution. What are the implications to believers if evolution is correct? What are the implications to non-believers if creationism is correct? Is there a middle ground?

Essays

1. Was Abraham a man of faith? Contrast events from Abraham's life where he moved by faith and events where he moved by his reason (Genesis 12–23).

2. Compare the Passover (Exodus 12 and 13) to Jesus' crucifixion and resurrection.

3. Describe the Jewish dietary laws (Leviticus 11, 17, Deuteronomy 14). To what extent do these laws have merit in light of recent scientific knowledge? Support your answer.

4. Describe the Jewish system for handling a deliberate or accidental killing of a person by another (Numbers 35, Deuteronomy 19). Compare to modern legal systems.

5. Describe the blessings and cursings associated with God's covenant (Deuteronomy 28). Compare with specific examples from the history of Israel in the books of Joshua and Judges.

6. Discuss the short term and long term effects to Israel of other nations remaining in the Promised Land. Does this foretell aspects of a believer's walk? Support your answer.

7. Discuss the remarkable events leading up to the birth of Jesus. Had you been there during that time, describe how you would have reacted to the angel's words and to the pregnancy.

8. Describe the progression of events and teachings that hardened the hearts of the religious leaders toward Jesus.

Unit 1 Beginnings

1. How was Jesus part of creation?

_____

_____

_____

  To whom do you suppose the word "us" refers to in Genesis 1:26?

_____

2. What were the results of Adam and Eve falling into temptation? (See also Romans 5.)

_____

_____

_____

3. Why do you suppose Abel's offering was accepted and Cain's offering was rejected?

_____

_____

_____

4. What was the sign of God's covenant with Noah?

_____

5. True or false: When God called Abram to leave his country, did Abram know where he was going?

_____

6. God gave Abram a new name, _____ , which meant

_____ .

7. Which of Abraham's sons was chosen to inherit the promise?

_____

8. Hebrews 11 tells us the following: Abraham believed that, had he sacrificed Isaac, God would do what?

_____

_____

9. What was the plan of Abraham's servant to find a wife for Isaac?

_____

_____

_____

10. Name two ways Jacob was changed after wrestling all night with the angel from God.

_____

_____

_____

11. From Psalm 1, what should we avoid?

_____

_____

What should we seek?

_____

_____

What are the benefits?

_____

_____

Unit 2 Israel in Egypt

1. Three different times Joseph was put in charge of his master's domain. Who were his three masters?

_____

_____

_____

   How long did it take the cupbearer to remember Joseph to Pharaoh?

_____

2. Why did Jacob keep Benjamin from going with his brothers on their first grain-buying trip to Egypt?

_____

_____

_____

   What eventually caused Jacob to allow Benjamin to go with his brothers on their second grain-buying trip?

_____

_____

_____

3. The Messiah would come from which tribe?

_____

4. Genesis 50:20 tells us that God used the early wickedness against Joseph by his brothers for what eventual good?

_____

_____

5. How was the baby Moses delivered from Pharaoh's death sentence?

_____

_____

_____

6. What is the translation of "Yahweh"?

_____

What does this mean for us?

_____

_____

7. How can we protect ourselves with the blood smears of Jesus?

_____

_____

8. Acts 7 tells us that Moses lived his first _____ years in Egypt and

his next _____ years in Midian.

9. Considering that leaven (or yeast) is a symbol for sin in Scripture, what is the spiritual significance of Exodus 13:7?

_____

_____

10. Why were the Hebrews required to redeem (set apart) their firstborn sons and sacrifice their firstborn livestock?

_____

_____

11. From Psalm 8:4–6, the Hebrew word for "God" can be translated "angel". From Hebrews 2:1–9, to whom does this passage refer?

_____

What was the specific duration for "a little while"?

_____

Unit 3 Matthew

1. Why did Joseph want to quietly cancel his engagement to Mary?

_____

_____

2. How were Joseph and the Magi warned to change their respective plans?

_____

3. What happened immediately after Jesus was baptized and came up out of the water?

_____

_____

_____

4. List the eight pairs of godly attitudes and their associated blessings.

_____

_____

_____

_____

_____

_____

_____

5. When we ask God for forgiveness, what is our responsibility?

_____

_____

6. What hope do the kingdom of heaven parables give us?

_____

_____

7. From the two mass feedings, what was the lesson that the disciples missed?

_____

_____

_____

8. From Matthew, there were two times when an audible voice spoke from above. For each time this happened, when did it occur, and what was the message?

_____

_____

_____

_____

9. What is the last event that must be completed before the end will come?

_____

_____

10. What are the warnings from the parable of the ten virgins?

_____

_____

_____

11. What miraculous events took place immediately upon Jesus' death?

_____

_____

_____

12. What caused Joseph, the Jewish religious leader, to go public about his beliefs?

_____

_____

Unit 4 Israel at Sinai

1. Of the ten commandments, the first four deal with our relationship with

   _____ and the last six deal with our relationship with

   _____ .

2. Why did the LORD drive out the occupants of the Promised Land slowly?

   _____

   _____

3. How long did Moses stay on Mount Sinai?

   _____

4. Exodus 25:16 says "the testimony" was to be placed inside the Ark of the Covenant. What is this "testimony" more commonly known as? (Hint: see Hebrews 9:4.)

   _____

5. How often was the priest told to make atonement for the people upon the Ark?

   _____

6. The anointing oil was to anoint what things and what persons?

   _____

   _____

   _____

7. Before Moses came down from Mount Sinai, what did the people do?

   _____

   _____

   _____

What leader helped them?

_____

8. Why did there need to be a second set of tablets?

_____

_____

9. From 2 Corinthians 3, why did Moses put a veil over his face?

_____

_____

10. Once the tabernacle was completed, how did the LORD physically lead the people from place to place?

_____

_____

_____

11. What insects were permitted to be eaten?

_____

Who in the New Testament was known for eating such insects?

_____

12. From Acts 2, the Apostle Peter quoted from Psalm 16:8–11 to show that David the Psalmist prophesied about the Messiah (the Christ), that He would not be abandoned in

_____ nor would His flesh _____ .

Unit 5 Sentenced to the Desert

1. What was one of the LORD's plans for providing for the poor?

    _____

    _____

    _____

2. Give at least three examples from the Sermon on the Mount for replacing vengefulness.

    _____

    _____

    _____

3. How often were Sabbath years to occur?

    _____

    How often were Jubilee years to occur?

    _____

    What was to be released for the Jubilee?

    _____

    _____

4. What is common in the praises from David and Zacharias?

    _____

    _____

    How does Jesus protect us from Satan?

    _____

    _____

5. What was manna?

_____

_____

What was the peoples' complaint about manna?

_____

_____

How did the LORD react?

_____

_____

6. Compare the good report of Caleb and Joshua to the bad report of the other ten scouts.

_____

_____

_____

_____

_____

_____

7. What was promised to Caleb and Joshua?

_____

_____

What immediately happened to the ten scouts?

_____

_____

8. The Hebrews were sentenced to the desert for forty years. Why forty years?

_____

_____

9. Why was Moses denied from entering the Promised Land?

_____

_____

_____

10. What was the purpose for the bronze snake?

_____

_____

_____

_____

According to John 3:14, who does the bronze snake represent?

_____

Unit 6 Mark

1. Who said, "He must increase, but I must decrease"?

_____

2. Why did the people across the Sea of Galilee ask Jesus to leave?

_____

_____

3. Why did Herod keep his promise to the daughter of Herodias, although it meant the senseless killing of John the Baptist?

_____

_____

_____

4. What should we do when we feel like our prayers are not being heard and answered?

_____

_____

_____

5. What was the request from Jesus that the rich young man had difficulty following?

_____

_____

_____

6. If we fail to worship the Lord, what will take our place?

_____

_____

7. How can the Lord be a descendant of David?

_____

_____

_____

8. What does "Render Caesar's things to Caesar, and render God's things to God" mean?

_____

_____

_____

9. Whose offering at the treasury impressed Jesus and why?

_____

_____

_____

10. In the garden of Gethsemane, Jesus prayed intimately to His Father, asking Abba ("Daddy") to remove the cup from Him. What did the cup symbolize?

_____

_____

_____

_____

11. List the events of Jesus' arrest, trial, and crucifixion, that were predicted in Psalm 22.

_____

_____

_____

_____

_____

Unit 7 Preparation for Conquest

1. What caused Balaam's donkey to disobey him three times?

_____

_____

   Why did God let the donkey talk?

_____

_____

   Why did the angel of the LORD stop Balaam?

_____

_____

2. Who was selected to succeed Moses?

_____

   How did Moses acknowledge this in public?

_____

_____

_____

3. What are the two key commandments?

_____

_____

_____

4. From Deuteronomy 6:6–9, list the many ways we are to handle God's Word today.

_____

_____

_____

_____

5. From Deuteronomy 8:3, why did the LORD humble the Hebrews, allow them to be hungry, and feed them with manna in the desert?

_____

_____

Compare this with the devil's first temptation of Jesus in the desert (see Matthew 4).

_____

_____

_____

6. During what three festivals were all men to appear before God at His place of choosing?

_____

_____

_____

7. How were the people to judge a prophet's message?

_____

_____

8. What was the purpose for the cities of refuge?

_____

_____

_____

9. What was the minimum number of witnesses needed to convict a person of a crime?

_____

What was the significance of this during Jesus' trial before the Jewish religious leaders (see Matthew 26:59–61)?

_____

_____

10. From Deuteronomy 21:22–23, what was the "deadline" for Jesus dying on the cross and subsequent burial?

_____

Who fulfilled this Scripture for Jesus' body (see Luke 23:50–54)?

_____

From Galatians 3:13–14, what curse did Jesus take upon Himself on the cross?

_____

_____

From whom did He transfer this curse?

_____

Why did He do this?

_____

_____

11. From Psalm 29 (see also Psalm 96), how are we to "dress" when we approach the LORD in worship?

_____

_____

What does this mean to us?

_____

_____

_____

Unit 8 Inheritance Realized

1. What were the names of the mountains of blessings and cursings?

_____

What were the Hebrews commanded to do when they arrived there?

_____

_____

_____

2. What three things did God's people need to do in order to "choose life"?

_____

_____

_____

3. Who buried Moses?

_____

4. How did Moses die?

_____

_____

5. What were the two reasons the LORD stopped up the Jordan river, allowing the Hebrews to cross into the Promised Land on dry land?

_____

_____

_____

6. When did the manna stop?

_____

_____

7. The walls of Jericho fell down immediately after

_____

_____ .

8. How did Achan sin?

_____

_____

What was the impact upon the people?

_____

_____

9. What mistake did the Israelites make with the Gibeonites?

_____

_____

_____

10. How did the LORD fight for the Israelites against the Amorites?

_____

_____

_____

11. What activates God's forgiveness?

_____

_____

_____

Unit 9 Luke

1. Compare the responses of Zechariah and Mary to the angel Gabriel.

_____

_____

_____

_____

2. What happened when Mary greeted Elizabeth?

_____

_____

3. What did the twelve-year-old Jesus do after His parents found Him in the temple?

_____

_____

4. How did Jesus defend against the direct temptations by the devil?

_____

_____

5. What is the interpretation of the parable of the sower?

_____

_____

_____

_____

_____

6. In the parable of the good Samaritan, how did the Samaritan prove to be a neighbor to the dying Jewish man?

_____

_____

_____

How did this parable apply to its immediate audience?

_____

_____

_____

7. In the parables of the lost sheep, lost coin, and lost son, what are the ratios of lost item to remaining item(s)?

_____

_____

_____

8. Do you think the narrative regarding the rich man and Lazarus is a parable or a telling of actual events? Explain your answer.

_____

_____

_____

_____

9. What was Jesus' reaction when only one of the ten healed lepers returned and offered praise?

_____

_____

10. The two disciples whom Jesus joined on their trip to Emmaus did not recognize Him at first. What events led to their recognition of Him?

_____

_____

_____

_____

11. From Psalm 34, who do you suppose the "young lions" are?

_____

_____

_____

Semester 1 Exam

1. To whom do you suppose the word "us" refers to in Genesis 1:26?

_____

2. Hebrews 11 tells us the following: Abraham believed that, had he sacrificed Isaac, God would do what?

_____

_____

3. Genesis 50:20 tells us that God used the early wickedness against Joseph by his brothers for what eventual good?

_____

_____

4. Considering that leaven (or yeast) is a symbol for sin in Scripture, what is the spiritual significance of Exodus 13:7?

_____

_____

5. What happened immediately after Jesus was baptized and came up out of the water?

_____

_____

_____

6. What are the warnings from the parable of the ten virgins?

_____

_____

_____

7. How often was the priest told to make atonement for the people upon the Ark?

_____

8. From 2 Corinthians 3, why did Moses put a veil over his face?

_____

_____

9. Give at least three examples from the Sermon on the Mount for replacing vengefulness.

_____

_____

_____

10. What was the purpose for the bronze snake?

_____

_____

_____

_____

From John 3:14, who does the bronze snake represent?

_____

11. Who said, "He must increase, but I must decrease"?

_____

_____

12. What was the request from Jesus that the rich young man had difficulty following?

_____

_____

13. What are the two key commandments?

_____

_____

_____

14. During what three festivals were all men to appear before God at His place of choosing?

_____

_____

_____

15. What three things did God's people need to do in order to "choose life"?

_____

_____

_____

16. What mistake did the Israelites make with the Gibeonites?

_____

_____

_____

17. Compare the responses of Zechariah and of Mary to the angel Gabriel.

_____

_____

_____

_____

18. What was Jesus' reaction when only one of the ten healed lepers returned and offered praise?

_____

_____

_____

Semester 2
Activities

1. **Presentation:** Prepare a multi-chart (or computer-based) presentation showing the history of the Israelites under the judges. Include the cycles of subjugation and freedom.

2. **Collage:** Create a collage about the various seasons listed in Ecclesiastes 3.

3. **Journal:** For one of Jesus' disciples of your choice, write a journal of major events as seen from his eyes.

4. **Maps:** Draw one or more maps depicting the travels of Jesus during His ministry. Identify locations of major teachings, healings, and miracles.

5. **Script**: Adapt the events surrounding the death and resurrection of Jesus into a script for a television news program.

6. **Report:** What does the Bible say about homosexuality? How ought the church handle this issue? How do you think Jesus would treat homosexuals? Prepare a written report that describes your position and provide support. See Romans 1:26–27.

Essays

1. Since Satan is subject to God and needed to receive permission from God to afflict Job (Job 1–2), was God ultimately responsible for Job's troubles? Support your answer.

2. Discuss events in Samuel's life that demonstrated his integrity. What important contributions did he make to the history of Israel?

3. God described David as a man after His own heart (Acts 13:22). Discuss events from David's life that supported this. How do the events surrounding Bathsheba fit in?

4. The expression "all is vanity" (or meaningless) is found repeatedly in Ecclesiastes. Contrast the things the author considered to be meaningful to those he considered to be meaningless. Do you agree with the author? Support your answer.

5. Compare and contrast the gospel of John to the three synoptic gospels. What major events are common to all four? What major events are unique to John? How do you account for these differences? Support your answer.

6. Describe key events in the New Testament that helped fulfill Joel's prophecy of the outpouring of the Holy Spirit (Joel 2:28–32).

7. Contrast the ministries of Peter and of Paul in the book of Acts. Include the impact each made at the Jerusalem council (Acts 15).

8. Discuss the key points of Paul's presentation of the gospel in Romans 1–8.

Unit 10 When the Judges Governed

1. Why did the LORD stop driving out the other nations from the Promised Land?

_____

_____

2. What was Ehud's "message from God" for the king of Moab?

_____

_____

_____

3. Who were the two important women from Judges 4?

_____

   What did they do?

_____

_____

4. Where did the angel of the LORD find Gideon?

_____

_____

5. For what reason did the LORD reduce the size of Gideon's army on two occasions?

_____

_____

Why do you suppose the LORD kept those who knelt to drink and dismissed those who lapped with their tongues (Judges 7:5–6)?

_____

_____

_____

6. What was the terrible result of the vow that Jephthah made to the LORD to deliver the Ammonites to him?

_____

_____

7. What were the key Nazarite vows?

_____

_____

Which of these vows had special significance to Samson, and why?

_____

_____

8. What was the epitaph to Samson's life that is recorded in Scripture?

_____

_____

9. What was the role of the kinsman-redeemer (see Deuteronomy 25:5–7)?

_____

_____

10. When Ruth went to glean in Boaz's field, what special things did Boaz do for Ruth?

_____

_____

_____

_____

What important person was directly descended from Ruth and Boaz?

_____

11. From Psalm 40, what is promised to him who waits patiently for the LORD?

_____

_____

_____

_____

Unit 11 Job

1. From Job 1, how did God describe Job to Satan?

_____

_____

What did Satan say Job would do when faced with adversity?

_____

_____

2. What were the first four calamities that happened to Job?

_____

_____

_____

_____

    How did Job react?

_____

_____

3. From Job 2, what else happened to Job?

_____

    How did Job react?

_____

_____

4. How are we to respond to God's discipline?

_____

5. From Job 19, considering all that Job had suffered, what was his remarkable cry of triumph?

_____

    When did Job expect to see this fulfilled?

_____

_____

6. From Job 31, what sins did Job list that he had not committed?

_____

_____

_____

What was Job's challenge to God?

_____

_____

7. In God's first speech (Job 38–39), what things in the universe did He list that testify of Him?

_____

_____

What animals did He list that testify of Him?

_____

_____

What was Job's response?

_____

8. In God's second speech (Job 40–41), what two creatures did He describe to illustrate His power?

_____

What was Job's response?

_____

9. What action by Job occurred immediately prior to God restoring his fortunes?

_____

10. What do other Scriptures testify regarding Job (see Ezekiel 14:12–20 and James 5:11)?

_____

11. What can we learn from the deer?

_____

_____

Unit 12 John

1. How did John the Baptist answer the question, "Who are you?"

_____

_____

2. List the different ways the Samaritan woman at Jacob's well referred to Jesus as their conversation proceeded.

_____

_____

3. When confronted with the woman who had committed adultery, Jesus asked her accusers to meet what qualification in order to carry out capital punishment?

_____

_____

Who met this criteria?

_____

_____

When her accusers left, what did Jesus do?

_____

_____

4. For the man born blind, what is the reason Jesus gave for his blindness?

_____

_____

What did Jesus use to heal him?

_____

_____

When the man learned of the lordship of Jesus, what did he do?

_____

_____

5. Who are the other sheep who are not of the good shepherd's immediate fold?

_____

_____

6. Regarding Lazarus, what is the reason Jesus gave for his sickness (which led directly to his death, but later to his being raised from the dead)?

_____

_____

7. Why did Jesus weep?

_____

_____

_____

8. What did Jesus pray for all believers?

_____

_____

_____

_____

_____

9. List the numerous ways that Pilate tried to avoid sentencing Jesus to death.

_____

_____

_____

_____

_____

10. To guide Peter to full restoration after his previous denials, how many times did Jesus ask Peter to declare his love for Him?

_____

11. From Psalm 48, what are some of the attributes of the "city of our God"?

_____

_____

_____

_____

What is the name of this city and what is its ultimate destiny (see Revelation 21)?

_____

_____

_____

Unit 13 Samuel and Saul

1. Give an example of Eli's poor spiritual leadership.

_____

_____

_____

2. What happened to the Philistines after they had captured the Ark?

_____

_____

How was the Ark returned to Israel?

_____

_____

How did the Philistines learn that the God of Israel had caused them such calamity?

_____

_____

_____

3. After Samuel anointed Saul with oil, what did Saul do with the group of prophets in Gibeah?

_____

4. From 1 Samuel 15, how did Saul sin?

_____

_____

What was the result?

_____

_____

5. From Acts 13:21–22, what was God's reason for choosing David to replace Saul as king?

_____

_____

6. David's harp playing had what effect on Saul?

_____

_____

7. What credentials did David tell Saul that convinced him to permit David to fight Goliath?

_____

_____

How much ammunition did David need to defeat Goliath?

_____

How did David keep his word regarding Goliath's head?

_____

_____

8. In the cave of Adullam, David's army consisted of 400 men with at least one of what three problems?

_____

_____

_____

9. David spared Saul's life two times. What things did he take from Saul that he later used to show he meant Saul no harm?

_____

_____

_____

   Why did David spare Saul's life?

_____

_____

10. David wrote Psalm 51 after his sin with Bathsheba was exposed by Nathan the prophet. This psalm can be divided into three sections which show the path David followed to find restoration to the LORD. Identify these three sections.

_____

_____

_____

Unit 14 David

1. When the oxen that were hauling the Ark stumbled, Uzzah steadied the Ark with his hand. Immediately, he was struck dead by God. Why?

_____

_____

2. What did David do when the Ark was finally carried into Jerusalem?

_____

_____

What was Michal's reaction?

_____

_____

What was David's response?

_____

_____

How did Michal's actions impact her life?

_____

_____

3. How was David's Tent different from the Tabernacle and the Temple?

_____

_____

_____

4. From 2 Samuel 11, compare and contrast David's integrity to Uriah's integrity.

_____

_____

_____

_____

_____

5. What were the consequences of David's adultery and subsequent sins?

_____

_____

_____

What was David's reaction when the child died?

_____

_____

Who was the mother's next child?

_____

6. How did Absalom steal the hearts of the people away from David?

_____

_____

_____

7. As David fled from Jerusalem, who were the five members of the spy ring he sent back to Jerusalem to conspire against Absalom?

_____

_____

8. What was Ahithophel's advice to Absalom regarding David and his warriors?

_____

_____

_____

What was Hushai's advice?

_____

_____

Whose advice did Absalom take?

_____

What did Ahithophel do next?

_____

What did Hushai do next?

_____

_____

9. How did Absalom die?

_____

_____

_____

_____

10. From 1 Chronicles 22, why was Solomon put in charge of building the temple instead of David?

_____

_____

_____

Unit 15 Acts

1. What were Jesus' last instructions just prior to His ascension?

_____

_____

_____

_____

_____

How did Jesus ascend?

_____

_____

After His ascension, the two angels said He would return how?

_____

_____

2. List the physical events which occurred when the Holy Spirit moved on the Day of Pentecost.

_____

_____

_____

_____

_____

3. What were the main points in Peter's sermon that followed?

_____

_____

_____

_____

What happened afterward?

_____

_____

4. What did Stephen say that caused the Sanhedrin to do him violence?

_____

_____

Why did this anger them so much?

_____

_____

In the narrative, what key figure appeared for the first time?

_____

How did the overall climate change after the stoning of Stephen?

_____

_____

_____

5. Describe the events of Saul's conversion from the viewpoint of Ananias.

_____

_____

_____

_____

6. What was the meaning of the visions that Peter had about a sheet full of animals?

_____

_____

How did the Lord confirm this?

_____

_____

7. What did God reveal to Paul after he appeared before the Sanhedrin?

_____

_____

8. Why did Paul remain under arrest for two full years under Governor Felix's rule?

_____

_____

_____

9. Why did Paul appeal to Caesar?

_____

_____

10. On the ship, the angel told Paul something about his future. What was it?

_____

_____

11. From Psalm 61:2, what do you suppose David meant when he said, "Lead me to the rock that is higher than I"?

_____

_____

_____

Unit 16 Solomon

1. When given one wish from God, for what did Solomon ask?

_____

_____

Besides granting this wish, what also did God promise Solomon?

_____

_____

2. How did Solomon determine which of the two prostitutes claiming to be the mother of the same child was the real mother?

_____

_____

_____

_____

3. Solomon took _____ years to build the Temple of the LORD and

_____ years to build his own palace.

4. Describe the "worship team" (musicians and orchestra) assembled for the placing of the Ark into the temple.

_____

_____

_____

_____

   After the Ark was placed into the temple, why were the priests unable to carry out their duties?

_____

_____

5. The LORD said He would hear from heaven if His people would do what four things?

_____

_____

_____

_____

6. In Matthew 12:42, Jesus made reference to the meeting of the Queen of Sheba (South) and Solomon. What did Jesus think about her, and why?

_____

_____

_____

7. Who eventually led Solomon astray from God?

_____

_____

8. Considering that in Old Testament times, everyone went to Sheol after death; why should our goal be to complete every task to the best of our abilities?

_____

_____

9. In the conclusion of Ecclesiastes, what are each person's duties?

_____

_____

What will God respond?

_____

_____

10. The Song of Songs (or Song of Solomon) can be interpreted in a simple way

as an ancient poem celebrating _____ .

11. From Psalm 65:8–11, list the signs of God that cause people to stand in awe.

_____

_____

_____

_____

Unit 17 Proverbs

1. What does the book of Proverbs teach us?

_____

_____

_____

_____

2. What is the lesson to be learned from the ant?

_____

_____

_____

3. What are seven things the LORD hates?

_____

_____

_____

_____

4. To what is a beautiful woman without discretion compared?

_____

_____

5. In Proverbs 18:24, why do you suppose "a man of too many friends [or acquaintances] comes to ruin"?

_____

_____

Who is "a friend who sticks closer than a brother"?

_____

6. To what is being gracious to, or giving to, a poor person the same as?

_____

What is promised that the LORD will do in return?

_____

7. How does a young man set himself apart?

_____

_____

8. We are warned not to commit either of two specific crimes, or the Redeemer will defend our victims. What are these crimes?

_____

_____

_____

_____

9. Compare Proverbs 25:21–22 and Romans 12:17–21. Why should you "never take your own revenge"?

_____

_____

How should we treat an enemy?

_____

_____

10. What are four things too wonderful to understand?

_____

_____

_____

_____

11. Psalm 69:4–9 is quoted twice in the Gospel of John, during Jesus' first trip to Jerusalem, and during His last trip to Jerusalem. What are these two quotes, and to what events of Jesus' ministry do they refer?

_____

_____

_____

_____

_____

Unit 18 Romans

1. What three reasons did Paul give for wanting to visit the believers in Rome?

_____

_____

_____

_____

2. Describe Paul's internal conflict with sin.

_____

_____

_____

_____

_____

_____

_____

      Who will rescue us from our bodies of death?

_____

3. Where is there no condemnation?

_____

4. Which law now rules over the other: the law of the Spirit of life or the law of sin and death?

_____

Why?

_____

_____

_____

What is our obligation?

_____

_____

5. Within the greater scriptural context, what are the things that God causes to work together for our good (Romans 8:26–28)?

_____

_____

6. List the things that cannot separate us from the love of God in Christ Jesus.

_____

_____

_____

_____

7. How did the Gentiles (non-Jews) obtain righteousness?

_____

How did the Jews fail to obtain righteousness?

_____

_____

8. To become saved, what do you need to do with your mouth and what do you need to do with your heart?

_____

_____

How does faith come?

_____

_____

9. What is the meaning of the olive tree and the branches?

_____

_____

_____

_____

_____

_____

10. What sacrifice from us is acceptable to God?

_____

How can we prove what the will of God is for us?

_____

_____

11. List the seven motivational gifts, which "differ according to the grace given to us."

_____

_____

_____

_____

12. How can we fulfill the Law of Moses?

_____

Semester 2 Exam

1. Why did the LORD stop driving out the other nations from the Promised Land?

_____

_____

2. What was the epitaph to Samson's life that is recorded in Scripture?

_____

_____

3. From Job 19, considering all that Job had suffered, what was his remarkable cry of triumph?

_____

_____

    When did Job expect to see this fulfilled?

_____

_____

4. What action by Job occurred immediately prior to God restoring his fortunes?

_____

_____

5. Regarding Lazarus, what is the reason Jesus gave for his sickness (which led directly to his death, but later to his being raised from the dead)?

_____

_____

6. To guide Peter to full restoration after his previous denials, how many times did Jesus ask Peter to declare his love for Him?

_____

7. From Acts 13:21–22, what was God's reason for choosing David to replace Saul as king?

_____

_____

8. What credentials did David tell Saul that convinced him to permit David to fight Goliath?

_____

_____

How much ammunition did David need to defeat Goliath?

_____

How did David keep his word regarding Goliath's head?

_____

_____

9. What did David do when the Ark was finally carried into Jerusalem?

_____

_____

What was Michal's reaction?

_____

_____

What was David's response?

_____

_____

How did Michal's actions impact her life?

_____

_____

10. From 1 Chronicles 22, why was Solomon put in charge of building the temple instead of David?

_____

_____

11. List the physical events which occurred when the Holy Spirit moved on the Day of Pentecost.

_____

_____

_____

_____

12. What was the meaning of the visions that Peter had about a sheet full of animals?

_____

_____

How did the Lord confirm this?

_____

_____

_____

13. When given one wish from God, for what did Solomon ask?

_____

_____

    Besides granting this wish, what also did God promise Solomon?

_____

_____

14. In the conclusion of Ecclesiastes, what are each person's duties?

_____

_____

    What will be God's response?

_____

_____

15. What does the book of Proverbs teach us?

_____

_____

_____

_____

16. In Proverbs 18:24, why do you suppose "a man of too many friends [or acquaintances] comes to ruin"?

_____

_____

    Who is "a friend who sticks closer than a brother"?

_____

17. Where is there no condemnation?

_____

18. List the things that cannot separate us from the love of God in Christ Jesus.

_____

_____

_____

_____

41563379R00040

Made in the USA
San Bernardino, CA
15 November 2016